sdr & हीरे धीरे

Sensational Revelation of

Professor Lorry, the Discoverer of

THE LORNS,

Proves that

SANTA CLAUS EXISTS!

by Pal

Sacer Equestris Aureus Ordo

ISBN- 13: 978-0615740676
ISBN-10: 0615740677

Sacer Equestris Aureus Ordo Inc.
Children Books division
PO B. 411, West Long Branch, NJ 07764

To my grandsons
Nicholas and Marcus,
Nonno

One Christmas Eve, Nicholas, Marcus, and Victoria asked Nonno-Grandfather, "Does Santa Claus exist?"

Nonno told his grandchildren, "There is One-Pure-Love. It is when one loves without wanting anything from the person loved. My dear children that Love is like a Gentle-Wind, which very few realize it exists and even fewer experience it all the time.

Everyone knows Desire. That too is like a wind, the ancient Greeks called it Eros.[1]

Everyone knows that War exists. It is similar to a wild wind, called Mars by the ancient Romans.[2]

Who does not experience Passion, Hate, Greed, Anger, etc. They are all like winds. Ancient people gave them different names. No one would deny them. Actually, if anyone says that Desire, War and the others do not exist, s/he would immediately be considered mad and countless historical proofs would be offered."

"Nonno, why they are called winds?" asked Nicholas with his marveled big eyes.

Nonno, caressing the child's head, answered, "Naturally, these types of winds are not the atmospheric ones. Each one of these winds is a strong impulse, which, like a wind, blows the mind away. When any of those winds blows, it takes one away from itself, in different far lands, like a garden of earthly delights.[3]

When one flies there, it is difficult to find the way back home. Once in that new place, everyone becomes a stranger in its own true Self. Those who go there forget their self, their real mother, father and country. There, they learn to speak a new language and the new locality becomes their new home. When asked, they say -- This is my true home, no other one exists.--"

"Don't they ever feel homesick?" asked Marcus, with sad eyes.

Nonno replied, "Oh, yes they do, like all of us. Nevertheless, they immediately dismiss it saying, -- What is this nonsense! We must be realistic. This is the only truth.

War is true,[4] who can disagree;

anger is true, [5] who can negate it;

hate is true, who can deny it;[6]

etc. All other things are only for ignorant babies.--"

Nonno got up to make some hot cocoa for everyone.

When done, they sat by the fireplace to drink the chocolate.

Victoria puzzled asked, "How many winds of war are there?"

Nonno replied, "There is only one wind of war and only one. In fact, the wind-of-war is always the same identical wind either when fought with swords,

in ancient times[7] or when fought with cannons and bombs

in modern times.[8] That wind has never changed; it has always been the will to kill win and conquer. The same can be said for all the other single winds I mentioned before."

"Oh! Then, there are no good winds in the world?" exclaimed Victoria with a certain fear in her voice.

"No!" Nonno assured her, "First, you must understand the difference between

HOKUSAI

atmospheric wind[9] and winds of the psyche, where the

mind is blown away by passions.[10] Both, the wind of the atmosphere and the winds of the mind exist. In the atmosphere, the wind remains always the same. The wind is the wind.

For humans, its effects can be good or bad. For them the wind is bad when it destroys and kills, like a

tornado.[11]

It is good when it produces useful things. The good wind

blows around the World feeding

windmills,[12] they produce flour for bread;

wind-turbines,[13] they produce electricity for light bulbs;

and wind-organs,[14] they produce nice sounds for the ear;

etc.

You understand very well that mills, turbines and

organs are not the wind. Nobody ever says that a mill is

the wind. That would be very silly. Only Don Quixote, a

fantastic silly knight, fought windmills considering them

had giants.[15]

Don Quixote and the Windmill
Drawing by Gustave Doré

"That is really silly." The children said laughing.

"Nevertheless, mills, turbines and organs without the wind would be useless. More so, nobody says that the wind does not exist because we cannot see it," Nonno concluded.

Promptly, Nicholas replied, "Yes, but we can feel the wind blowing on our face and in our hair."

Nonno fixed his spectacles on his nose, took a sip of cocoa from his big jug and continued,

"That is very true. It is like everyone having felt, at least once in a lifetime, the One-Gentle-Wind-of-Pure-Love. Nobody ever saw Love. You feel love for your mommy and daddy, but you cannot see that love. This does not mean it does not exist."

"That is so true!" The kids replied with one voice.

And Nonno reinforced, "Today, most people, because they have not seen love, say with a loud voice, -- Pure-Love does not exist!-"

All looked at Nonno in disbelief and said, "Yes, I know Love exists!"

"Long time ago," continued Nonno, "people were as savvy as you are, my dear grandchildren. They had no trouble recognizing the beauty of that love. Today, people think they can buy everything

at the supermarket.

Therefore, if they do not find love there on the shelves, they immediately say that it does not exist."

Very worried, Victoria asked, "Nonno, does this mean that we have no more love?"

Assuring, Nonno replied, "No, my dear ones, in ancient time, people from the North recognized that there is such Pure-Love and they called it Odin.[16]

This was only a name given to the truly existing Gentle-

Wind-of-Pure-Love that asks nothing in return.

Native American called it

Potlatch, Pure-Giving,[17] Hindus and Buddhist affirm that

only giving all away one can be truly free. The Bible says

that God accepted this type of sacrifice from Abel and Abraham.

However, the supermarket shoppers did not understand it. If they only had looked into their own hearts they would have found three kings bringing very valuable gifts to baby

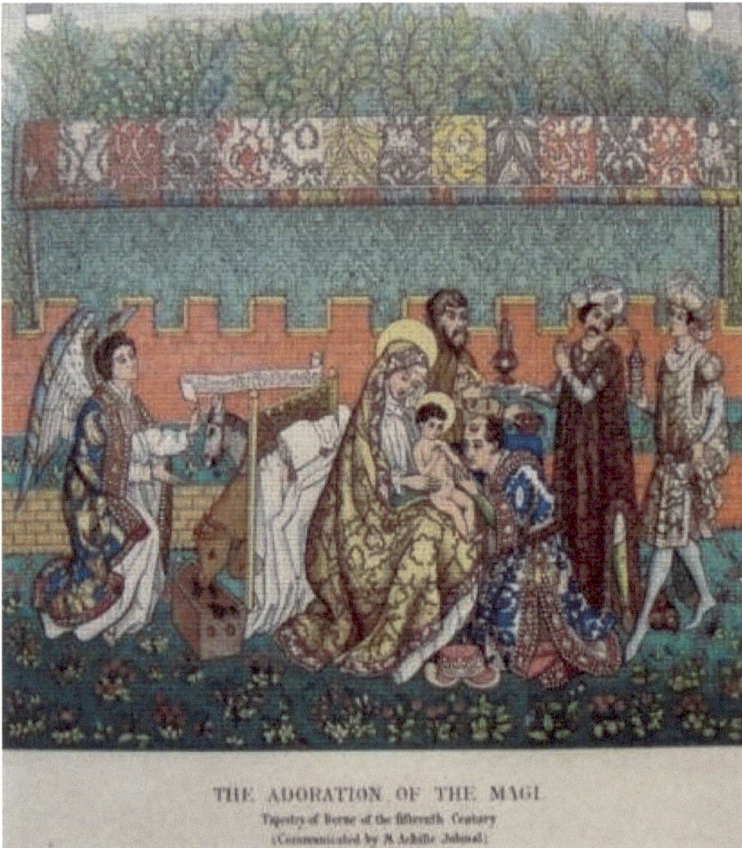

THE ADORATION OF THE MAGI
Tapestry of Berne of the fifteenth Century
(Communicated by M. Achille Jubinal)

Jesus in a manger.[18]

When he grew up, Jesus himself encouraged to give to the poor out of love. This is giving without expecting anything in return. This loving giving exists; it is a real wind that blows the mind to love others as oneself."

"Do we know of anyone's mind that has ever been blown away by that real wind of love?" Asked Nicholas perplexed.

"Yes," quickly answered Nonno, "One of them was Saint Nicholas of Myra,[19] a Christian bishop who lived many hundreds of years ago. He was so full of that existing Gentle-Wind-of-Pure-Love that he gave away all he had to feed hungry kids, never asking anything in return."

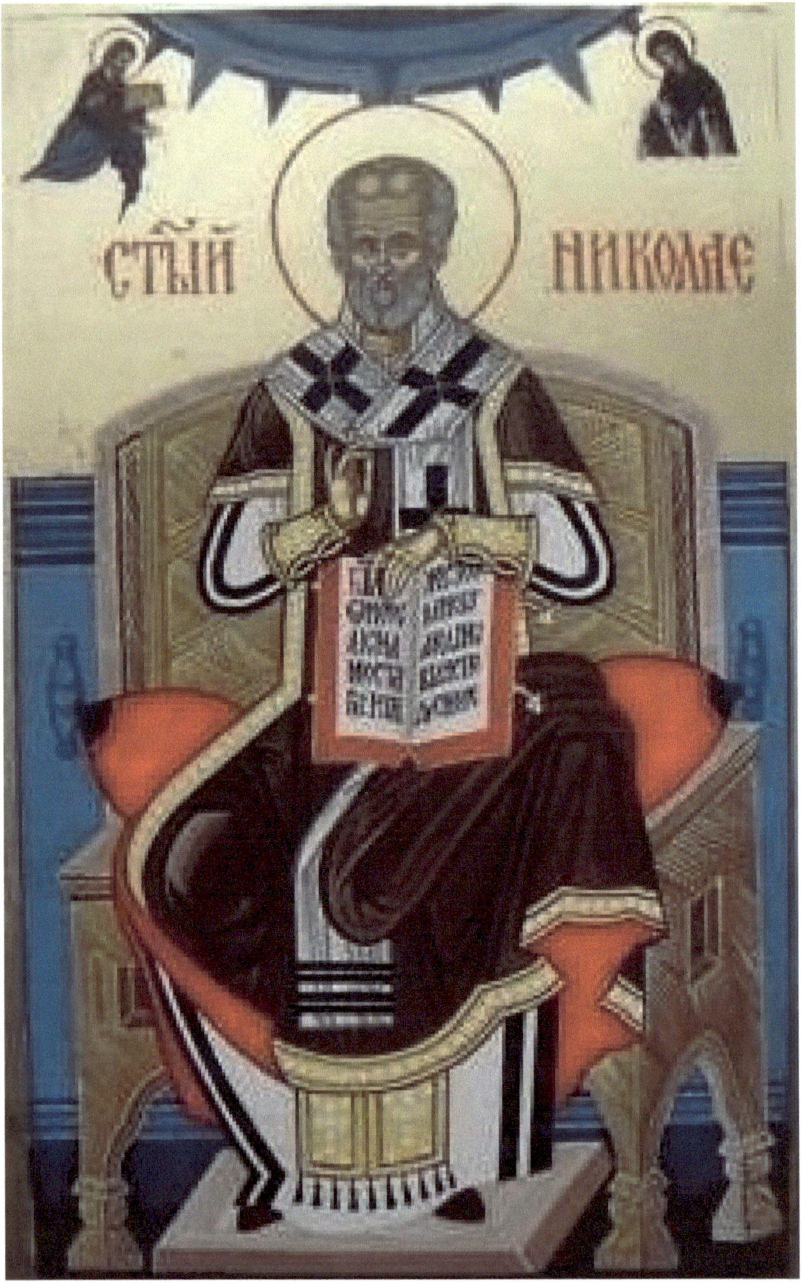
СТЫЙ
НИКОЛАЕ

The children asked, "Nonno tell us what ever happened to that Gentle-Wind-of-Pure-Love?"

Nonno, becoming very serious, replied, "Today, that One-Gentle-Wind-of-Pure-Love leads all the mommies and daddies of the world to fulfill the wishes of their kids and see the smile on their faces when they unwrap presents. They do this because they love their kids very very much, while they ask nothing in return."

"But this is like Santa Claus during Christmas." The children observed.

"Yes," replied Nonno, "Santa Claus is the name given, in some parts of the world, to that One-Gentle-Wind-of-Pure-Love, which Truly-Exists in the hearts of all mommies and daddies.

Mommies and daddies in the World are Santa Claus. However, as the windmills blown by the wind, they are enveloped by that Pure-Love, the one, the real, the existing Santa Claus and produce joy for all kids around the World. Therefore, let that One-Gentle-Wind-of-Pure-Love take over your heart and become the One-Truly-Existing-Santa-Claus."

"I <u>am</u> hungry," said Nonno, "Let us all go to dinner now."

As everyone sat at the table, Nonno continued, "You see, everyone <u>is</u> hungry, at dinner time. Nonno <u>is</u> hungry, Nonna (grandma) <u>is</u> hungry, daddy <u>is</u> hungry, mommy <u>is</u> hungry and those who love you <u>are</u> hungry. However, hunger <u>is only one</u>, identical for everyone. No one can say, hunger is Nonno, hunger is nonna, hunger is daddy, hunger is mommy or hunger is all those who love you. BUT, ANYONE CAN BE HUNGRY.

In the same way, at Christmas time, Nonno <u>is</u> Santa, nonna <u>is</u> Santa, daddy <u>is</u> Santa, mommy <u>is</u> Santa, and all those who love you <u>are</u> Santa.

From his part, Santa <u>exists</u> and <u>is</u> only one. Therefore, Santa is not Nonno, Santa is not nonna, Santa is not daddy, and Santa is not mommy.

REMEMBER, REMEMBER, REMEMBER

<u>SANTA IS ALL THOSE WHO LOVE YOU</u>

AND

<u>EVERY MOMENT OF YOUR LIFE IS CHRISTMAS</u>."

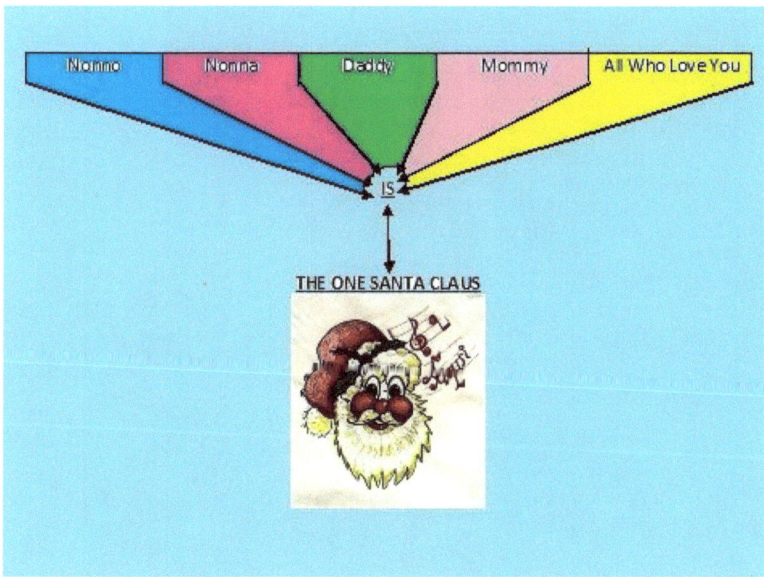

NOTES

[1] Eros, image public domain, Wikipedia, File: Eros Farnese Man Napoli 6353.jpg.
(http://en.wikipedia.org/wiki/File:Eros_Farnese_MAN_Napoli_6353.jpg).
[2] Mars, image public domain, Wikipedia, File: Mars Porte de Paris 12018.jpg.
(http://commons.wikimedia.org/wiki/File:Mars_Porte_de_Paris_12018.jpg).
[3] The Garden of Earthly Delights by Bosch. image public domain, Wikipedia, File: The
Garden of Earthly Delights by Bosch High Resolution
2.jpg,
(http://commons.wikimedia.org/wiki/File:The_Garden_of_Earthly_Delights_by_Bosch_
High_Resolution_2.jpg).
[4] War, image public domain, Wikipedia, File:Battle of Fort Fisher.jpg.
http://en.wikipedia.org/wiki/File:Battle_of_Fort_Fisher.jpg
[5] "Anger" image public domain, Wikipedia, File:Angry man.svg,
http://commons.wikimedia.org/wiki/File:Angry_man.svg
[6] "Hate" Free Software Foundation GNU Free Documentation License. File:Att-hate.svg,
http://commons.wikimedia.org/wiki/File:Att-hate.svg
[7] Alexander the Great, Battle of Issus. Image public domain, Wikipedia, File: Battle of
Issus.jpg,
(http://en.wikipedia.org/wiki/File:Battle_of_Issus.jpg).
[8] Atomic War oil on canvas.
[9] Japanese print.
[10] XVI-XVII century prints.
[11] Tornado, image public domain, Wikipedia, File: Dszpics1.jpg.
(http://en.wikipedia.org/wiki/File:Dszpics1.jpg).
[12] Windmill, the Free Software Foundation, GNU Free Documentation License,
File:Wilton2.jpg http://en.wikipedia.org/wiki/File:Wilton2.jpg.
[13] Wind turbines, Creative Commons image GNU Free Documentation License, Version
1.2, Wikipedia, File:Veladero 01.png,
(http://en.wikipedia.org/wiki/File:Veladero_01.png).
[14] Organ, Image public domain, Wikipedia, File:Portativ.jpg. (http
http://en.wikipedia.org/wiki/File:Portativ.jpg).
[15] Don Quixote fighting a windmill. Illustration by Dorè.
[16] Odin's portrait.
[17] Haida Indian, Potlatch Dance, ALASKA, 1905.
[18] Adoration of the Magi, Tapestry.
[19] Saint Nicholas, Byzantine Orthodox icon by Bulgarian painter Fiko Fikov;

www.ingramcontent.com/pod-product-compliance
Lightning Source LLC
Chambersburg PA
CBHW041806040426
42448CB00001B/53